On Money
Quotes of John D. Rockefeller, Sr.

Copyright © 2016 Michael Gesell
All rights reserved.
ISBN-13: 978-1537055039
ISBN-10: 1537055038

Dedicated to all hardworking people

I.

I had no ambition to make a fortune. Mere money-making has never been my goal, I had an ambition to build.

II.

The person who starts out simply with the idea of getting rich won't succeed; you must have a larger ambition. There is no mystery in business success. If you do each day's task successfully, and stay faithfully within these natural operations of commercial laws which I talk so much about, and keep your head clear, you will come out all right.

III.

Charity is injurious unless it helps the recipient to become independent of it.

IV.

Singleness of purpose is one of the chief essentials for success in life, no matter what may be one's aim.

V.

The ability to deal with people is as purchasable a commodity as sugar or coffee and I will pay more for that ability than for any other under the sun.

VI.

Every right implies a responsibility. Every opportunity, an obligation, every possession, a duty.

VII.

I would rather earn 1% off a 100 people's efforts than 100% of my own efforts.

VIII.

If your only goal is to become rich, you will never achieve it.

IX.

It is wrong to assume that men of immense wealth are always happy.

X.

The road to happiness lies in two simple principles; find what interests you and that you can do well, and put your whole soul into it - every bit of energy and ambition and natural ability you have.

XI.

Good management consists in showing average people how to do the work of superior people.

XII.

I believe in the dignity of labor, whether with head or hand; that the world owes no man a living but that it owes every man an opportunity to make a living.

XIII.

God gave me my money. I believe the power to make money is a gift from God to be developed and used to the best of our ability for the good of mankind. Having been endowed with the gift I possess, I believe it is my duty to make money and still more money and to use the money I make for the good of my fellow man according to the dictates of my conscience.

XIV.

I know of nothing more despicable and pathetic than a man who devotes all the hours of the waking day to the making of money for money's sake.

XV.

I always tried to turn every disaster into an opportunity.

XVI.

I do not think that there is any other quality so essential to success of any kind as the quality of perseverance. It overcomes almost everything, even nature.

XVII.

I can think of nothing less pleasurable than a life devoted to pleasure.

XVIII.

Do you know the only thing that gives me pleasure? It's to see my dividends coming in.

XIX.

If you want to succeed you should strike out on new paths, rather than travel the worn paths of accepted success.

XX.

The only question with wealth is, what do you do with it?

XXI.

I believe in the supreme worth of the individual and in his right to life, liberty and the pursuit of happiness.

XXII.

I believe that the law was made for man and not man for the law; that government is the servant of the people and not their master.

XXIII.

I believe that thrift is essential to well-ordered living and that economy is a prime requisite of a sound financial structure, whether in government, business or personal affairs.

XXIV.

I believe that the rendering of useful service is the common duty of mankind and that only in the purifying fire of sacrifice is the dross of selfishness consumed and the greatness of the human soul set free.

XXV.

I believe in the sacredness of a promise, that a man's word should be as good as his bond, that character—not wealth or power or position—is of supreme worth.

XXVI.

I believe that truth and justice are fundamental to an enduring social order.

XXVII.

Don't be afraid to give up the good to go for the great.

XXVIII.

I believe in an all-wise and all-loving God, named by whatever name, and that the individual's highest fulfillment, greatest happiness and widest usefulness are to be found in living in harmony with His will.

XXIX.

I believe that love is the greatest thing in the world; that it alone can overcome hate; that right can and will triumph over might.

XXX.

The secret to success is to do the common things uncommonly well.

XXXI.

A friendship founded on business is better than a business founded on friendship

XXXII.

I would rather hire a man with enthusiasm, than a man who knows everything.

XXXIII.

The most important thing for a young man is to establish a credit . . . a reputation, character.

XXXIV.

The ability to deal with people is as purchasable a commodity as sugar or coffee. And I will pay more for that ability than for any other in the world.

XXXV.

Next to doing the right thing, the most important thing is to let people know you are doing the right thing.

XXXVI.

A man has no right to occupy another man's time unnecessarily.

XXXVII.

I was early taught to work as well as play,
My life has been one long, happy holiday;
Full of work and full of play-
I dropped the worry on the way-
And God was good to me every day.

XXVIII.

If you want to succeed you should strike out on new paths, rather than travel the worn paths of accepted success.

XXXIX.

Nobody does anything if he can get anybody else to do it.

XL.

The only thing which is of lasting benefit to a man is that which he does for himself. Money which comes to him without effort on his part is seldom a benefit and often a curse.

XLI.

Competition is a sin.

XLII.

In the same way the failures which a man makes in his life are due almost always to some defect in his personality, some weakness of body, or mind, or character, will, or temperament. The only way to overcome these failings is to build up his personality from within, so that he, by virtue of what is within him, may overcome the weakness which was the cause of the failure. It is only those efforts the man himself puts forth that can really help him.

XLIII.

The day of combination is here to stay. Individualism has gone, never to return.

XLIV.

This Sunday School has been of help to me, greater perhaps than any other force in my Christian life, and I can ask no better things for you than that you, and all that shall come after you in this great band of workers for Christ, shall receive the same measure of blessedness which I have been permitted to have.

XLV.

Giving should be entered into in just the same way as investing. Giving is investing.

XLVI.

God gave me my money.

XLVII.

We can never learn too much of His will towards us, too much of His messages and His advice. The Bible is His word and its study gives at once the foundation for our faith and an inspiration to battle onward in the fight against the tempter.

XLVIII.

I believe it is a religious duty to get all the money you can, fairly and honestly; to keep all you can, and to give away all you can.

XLIX.

I believe the power to make money is a gift of God … to be developed and used to the best of our ability for the good of mankind. Having been endowed with the gift I possess, I believe it is my duty to make money and still more money and to use the money I make for the good of my fellow man according to the dictates of my conscience.

L.

When hard work goes out of style we may expect to see civilization totter and fall.

ABOUT JOHN D. ROCKEFELLER

John Davison Rockefeller Sr. (July 8, 1839 – May 23, 1937) was an American industrialist and philanthropist. He is considered to be the richest person in history. He revolutionized the petroleum industry and defined the structure of modern philanthropy. In 1870, he founded Standard Oil Company and actively ran it until he officially retired in 1897.

Rockefeller was also the founder of both the University of Chicago and Rockefeller University and funded the establishment of Central Philippine University in the Philippines. He advocated abstinence from alcohol and tobacco and was a proponent of women's rights. He was a devout and devoted Northern Baptist, and supported many church-based institutions. Although he was a merciless capitalist, religion was a guiding force throughout his life, and Rockefeller believed it to be the source of his success.

www.ingramcontent.com/pod-product-compliance
Lightning Source LLC
Chambersburg PA
CBHW071839200526
45169CB00020B/2006